Essential Skills for your
Brilliant Family Dog

Book 1

Why is my dog so growly?

Teach your fearful, aggressive, or reactive dog
confidence through understanding

Beverley Courtney

Books by the author

Essential Skills for a Brilliant Family Dog

Book 1 Calm Down! *Step-by-Step to a Calm, Relaxed, and Brilliant Family Dog*
Book 2 Leave it! *How to teach Amazing Impulse Control to your Brilliant Family Dog*
Book 3 Let's Go! *Enjoy Companionable Walks with your Brilliant Family Dog*
Book 4 Here Boy! *Step-by-step to a Stunning Recall from your Brilliant Family Dog*

Essential Skills for your *Growly* but Brilliant Family Dog

Book 1 **Why is my Dog so Growly?** *Teach your fearful, aggressive, or reactive dog confidence through understanding*
Book 2 **Change for your Growly Dog!** *Action steps to build confidence in your fearful, aggressive, or reactive dog*
Book 3 **Calm walks with your Growly Dog** *Strategies and techniques for your fearful, aggressive, or reactive dog*

Your free book is waiting for you!

Impulse Control is particularly valuable for the reactive and anxious dog. Get a head start with your training by developing astonishing self-control in your dog! Change your dog from quick on the trigger, to thoughtful and reflective.

Go now and get your step-by-step book absolutely free at
Brilliant Family Dog

Disclaimer

I have made every effort to make my teachings crystal clear, but we're dealing with live animals here (that's you, and your dog) and I can't see whether you're doing it exactly right. I am unable to guarantee success, as it depends entirely on the person utilising the training programs, strategies, tools, and resources.

What I do know is that this system works!

Nothing in these books should upset or worry your dog in any way, but if your dog has bitten or you fear he may bite, you should take action straight away:

1. Use a muzzle
2. Consult a specialist force-free trainer

"I am not a vet"

You'll see this statement dotted about the book. I am not a vet, but there are some things with a medical slant that I need to draw your attention to.

I do not wish to wake up one morning and find my front lawn covered with angry vets brandishing syringes and latex gloves. On medical matters, take your vet's advice. You may want to seek out a veterinary behaviourist who specialises in this area.

Any opinions I express are based on my best efforts to study the literature, from personal experience, and from case studies. Not gospel, in other words.

Many of the techniques I show you were not invented by me, but I add my own spin. There will be a little repetition of key points from book to book, to ensure that the new reader has some understanding, and serve as a reminder to the rest of us. Ideally all three books should be read in sequence.

All the photos in this book are of "real" dogs – either my own, or those of students and readers (with their permission). So the reproduction quality is sometimes not the best. I have chosen the images carefully to illustrate the concepts – so we'll have to put up with some fuzziness.

Contents

Introduction

Picture the scene: you're walking along the road with your dog when - horror of horrors! - another person with a dog appears at the end of the street.

You know what's about to happen.

You start to breathe faster, your heart rate speeds up, you clutch the lead tightly to you, keeping your dog's head close. By this time your dog is on full alert, wondering what on earth has frightened you so much.

And sure enough, it happens.

Your dog spots the other dog, and lunges forward on the lead, barking ferociously. You gasp out broken commands as you try to keep your feet on the pavement. You try to pin your dog against the wall as the other person marches by with their dog.

Did they just look down their nose at you? Did they shoot your dog a filthy look?

Now shame enters the mix. Your dog has behaved badly, you were quite unable to control him, and now you're condemned as a useless dog-owner with a nasty dog.

This walk has turned into a walk of shame and misery. Your dog is now on his toes, anxiously scanning for the next intruder to bark at. Your hands are sore, your throat is dry. You wish you could disappear into a hole in the ground.

Sound familiar?

The first thing to realise is that you are not alone!

There are lots of people who have dogs whom they love dearly - dogs who are a pleasure and delight about the house, calm, biddable, great with the kids. But as soon as they venture out of the door, the horns grow.

They seem to have a Jekyll and Hyde character - they're a house-angel, street-devil.

And you have tried everything and don't know what else to do.

Take heart! Help is at hand. I am going to help you to change things so that your dog will gain confidence, you will gain confidence, and walks will become an enjoyable pastime once more.

Why can I help you?

I, too, am one of those people with a dog who is wonderful at home - but outside was another story. Lacy's hackles would stand up like spines on a porcupine. She'd lunge and plunge, choking on her collar. She'd look for all the world as if she wanted to tear the other dog - or person - limb from limb. For all the dogs I've lived with, I'd never had this problem before.

What made this all so much worse was that I am a professional dog trainer! Someone who helps people get the best from their dog! Clearly I had a huge gap in my learning, and it was urgent that I plugged that gap as soon as possible. I needed to help my dog, and it was clear that there are plenty of other people out there wrestling with this largely misunderstood problem.

So I embarked on further studies. I devoured everything I could find that promoted a force-free approach to the problem. I already knew that the best way to interact with any animal (or person, for that matter) is by encouraging and rewarding the response you want, rather than demanding, commanding, and manipulating. I learnt why my dog was doing what she did, so I could reject anything that made life worse for her, or which debased my own humanity.

I could say my studies culminated with becoming a Certified Behavior Adjustment Training Instructor (CBATI), but that simply marked a stage in my learning. Every dog I work with has an individual history, an individual owner, and an individual personality. There's no one-size-fits-all. My learning deepens with each new dog.

Listening to these dogs' owners and studying the dogs themselves leads me to a bespoke training program for each one. And once you've read through these books you'll be able to choose what will work for you, and your dog - in your life.

Take care, though, if you are selecting strategies, not to throw out the baby with the bathwater! Try everything I offer you before making any decisions about what will or will not work in your case.

Solid results

It's important that you don't start blaming. "If only that dog hadn't attacked her," "That trainer taught me all wrong," "She had such a hard time in the shelter." What happened, happened. It's history. Start from where you are now and move forwards from there.

And my reactive dog? Lacy is 99% ok now, in any situation. She even comes to classes with me and acts as a demo dog. I know what will work for her, and when she's better staying home for the day. I'm always aware of how she perceives the world and its denizens, and I'm able to help her keep her cool and enjoy her life so much more - without asking too much of her.

You could write a whole book about each of the topics in these short books. Indeed those books have already been written, and you can find many in the Resources Section at the end of each book. If you like in-depth study, then go for it.

My plan is to give you a shortcut from where you are now with your dog to where you'd like to be - without having to buy a library of books and learn a new "language". Every trade and profession has its own jargon, and this can be very confusing, even daunting, for someone who just wants to know what to do!

I will work with you through the system that I have seen work time and again with many different clients and their very different dogs - in a surprisingly short space of time.

Look at what Scruffy's owners had to say:

> When we first contacted you for help with Scruffy, we were worried that we would have to put in place some extreme measures, or that we might not be able to alter his behaviour at all. In fact, his behaviour has greatly improved and this has happened much more quickly than we expected.
>
> Scruffy used to become frantic and scrape at the floor to get towards any dog he saw, even at a great distance. This was embarrassing and stressful.
>
> He is now able to look at other dogs and move away with us to continue his walk. *This is a massive improvement in just a few weeks*. It means that we no longer avoid dogs, but in fact go out looking for them so that we can work on his training. The tools you have given us have been simple to learn and easy to incorporate into our daily walks.
>
> We are all enjoying our walks a lot more than we used to, and are looking forward to continuing with the training and helping Scruffy to make even more progress. Thank you!

These three books stand alone, but are best consumed together, in order.

- The first tells you what's going on and why - and some of this may surprise you. It's essential to understand a problem before attempting to fix it. This section should bring you lots of "Aha!" moments.

- The second book goes into the detail of what you're going to change and how, what approaches will work best, and what you need to make it all work. Lots of Lessons in this section. And much of this will involve change for *you:* exciting!

- And the third gets you out there with your dog, enjoying a new way of walking and interacting with her, and making the scene at the start of this Introduction - mercifully! - a thing of the past. Lots more Lessons here, and Troubleshooting sections to cover all the "what ifs" you'll come up with.

My suggestion is to read through the book first so you know where you're going, then while your brain is filtering and processing this information, you can go back to the start and work through the Action Steps and Lessons with your dog.

For ease of reading, your dog is going to be a he or a she as the whim takes me. He and she will learn the exact same way and have similar responses. There will be just a few occasions when we're discussing only a male or a female, and that will be clear.

Now let's dive in, with a look at what on earth is going on with our dog.

Section 1

Reactivity - what is it?

Chapter 1

Sometimes Smidge's halo slips a little – but it's there!

What do we mean by this word "reactivity"? Basically, it means that your dog is reacting to his environment, but that instead of being able to assess the situation calmly, make good judgements, and move on, he's stuck in "See dog: bark!"

You may think your dog is weird - that one moment he's a happy dog inside the house, and as soon as you step outside he turns into a snarly monster. Imagine you're enjoying tea and cake at a friend's house. You're happy and relaxed. Then your friend takes you to see his reptile collection (Oh no!! Exactly what makes your skin crawl!). In that room full of snakes and lizards, do you feel as comfortable as you were in the tea-and-cake room? And when he opens the cage and offers you one to hold … that's when you may panic and need to get out of the room.

Have you ever felt anxious and jittery for some reason? Worried about an interview, perhaps, or waiting for news from the hospital. Every bang or squeak makes you jump! Imagine living in that state all the time.

And at the bottom of this is usually FEAR. The reason your dog is making such a hullabaloo at the sight of another dog (or person, bike, jogger, car, plastic bag, you-name-it) is because she's trying to keep it away from her. Putting on an Oscar-winning display of teeth, claws, and noise usually does the trick.

The other person or dog may think, "This is a nasty dog, I'm outa here," or you - in your embarrassment and confusion - take the dog away, or dive into someone's driveway till the other has passed. Either way, for your dog, the barking and lunging worked! The threat is no longer there!

Sometimes this response is totally misunderstood by the owner, who says, "He drags me towards every dog because he wants to play".

In a little while we'll be looking in detail at Dog Body Language. It's possible you are not recognising some of the things your dog is telling you! It will be much clearer when you've learnt his sophisticated method of communication.

Dogs do what works

I will be saying this over and over again. Your dog doesn't have a secret agenda to terrify the neighbourhood; she has no wish to fight with every dog she sees. All she wants is for the thing that's coming at her to go away. And she's discovered that her fear reaction of barking and prancing often works. So that's what she'll keep doing.

Until ... we show her another way to get the same result! Without anxiety, distress, and disarray.

Imagine a bunch of youths at each end of a street, hurling abuse at each other. They don't really want to close the gap and risk getting hurt! They just want to appear big enough to deter the other crowd from advancing towards them. The guy who is being restrained by his mates as he lunges towards someone - he often doesn't want to go through with his threat. If his mates let go he would have to find a way to leave without losing face.

Your dog is not aggressive, nasty, vicious - any of the names that passers-by may give her. She's just afraid.

If this comes as a surprise to you, have a look at other aspects of your dog - around the house for instance. Does she jump at loud bangs? Does she bark at visitors? Is she deeply suspicious of any new object in her environment, creeping up slowly to inspect it on tippy-toes with outstretched neck? Does she get distressed when she's left alone? Is it hard to brush her, or trim her feet?

All these can also be indicators of an anxious dog who is more likely to react to strange dogs, people, or things, when out.

And keep in mind that your dog can be afraid of anything at all. While many reactive dogs are reactive to other dogs, there are plenty who are just fine with other dogs, but terrified of traffic, or tractors, or people, or children …

But my dog's friendly!

Another reason some dogs become reactive is frustration. They may really want to meet every dog or person in the world and expect a good outcome. This may work when they're off-lead and able to get away (more about that later on), but it may also come apart quite quickly when the other dog doesn't welcome the intrusion, or is much bigger and bolder than your dog first thought.

Off-lead this can result in a panic response where your dog snaps and barks before running away. There is scope for this to go badly wrong, if the other dog joins in the fray. On-lead the frustration grows very quickly, as the dog does not have the freedom to do what he wants, and little impulse control to deal with these feelings. So he barks and lunges towards the other dog.

The symptoms are the same as for the fear-barker - though the underlying cause is slightly different. This dog's actions are often misunderstood by his owner, who fears they have an aggressive dog.

The frustrated dog may have poor social skills, racing up to a strange dog and hurling himself in their face, or on top of them. Imagine someone doing that to you in the street: you'd have a thing or two to say, I'm sure!

He may be stuck in puppyhood, thinking that racing up to every dog is ok. This dog needs to learn manners, just as our children do. We wouldn't accept behaviour from a teenager or adult that we'd accept from a three-year-old child. It would be most inappropriate. And yet many owners think it's ok that their dog should jump up at every dog they see, just because they think he's friendly.

Jekyll on-lead, Hyde off-lead?

I find a lot of people saying to me that their dog is only reactive on-lead, and that off-lead "he's fine!"

I can only say that I've never seen a dog-reactive dog who is "fine" off-lead.

A little study of dog body language will reveal a lot of signs of discomfort in this dog. The only advantage of being off-lead is that the dog can get away before things get out of hand. And because this is not possible when he's on-lead, we get the "fight or flight" result: b-a-r-k-i-n-g.

In this chapter we have learnt that

- Dogs who bark and lunge at other dogs are not necessarily aggressive
- Over-friendly dogs need to learn polite dog manners
- We may need to view our own dogs differently

Chapter 2

More factors in your dog's reactivity

While the main reasons for your dog kicking up are fear, fear, fear, and frustration, there are other contributory factors that make it more likely, that need to be approached.

A guardy nature

First of these is the guardiness of your dog. Many types of dog have been bred for generations to guard - property, people, flocks. One of the characteristics of their ability to be a good and effective guard dog is that they immediately notice anything that is out of place. A coyote on the horizon? A person who should not be there? A paper bag which should definitely not be there - unrecognisable and alive as it moves and flutters in the breeze.

This is known as sensitivity to Sudden Environmental Change (SEC), and you can see how it is a laudable trait in a dog you want for guard duty. But many people admire these dogs - typically, German Shepherd Dogs, all-purpose farm dogs like Kelpies and some Collies, flock guardians such as Pyrenean Mountain Dogs and Maremmas, farm-bred terriers in every shape and form who are bred to despatch vermin - and assume that the inherited traits and instinctive drives that made them what they are will evaporate once they are in their home as a pet.

Not so! They are part of the package. So we have to live with that or train new responses for our dog.

That's mine!

Any dog can be a resource guarder - it's not dependent on breed or type. It simply means that once they have something they value, they do not want to share it! This may be food, a bed, toys, tissues in the bin, balls in the park, or their greatest resource - their owner. Dogs who are reactive around their owner but not so bothered at a distance from them - or in their absence - are often thought to be protecting their owner. What they're actually protecting is their poor sorry selves. Their owner is the source of all good things in their universe, so no dog is going to get near!

Sometimes all it takes is for the owner to step away and take himself out of the picture for their dog to stop worrying about this. Such is the case with my resource-guardy mini poodle Coco, who can interact with new dogs far better when I'm not too close.

Resource guarding is something you need to address. The first essential is never to challenge a dog who is guarding something: you are likely to get bitten! This is not a case of the dog challenging your authority - he just has something he wants to keep! Teach him how to swap similar items - first low-value (to him) objects, then gradually working up till you can swap bones with him. Take things slowly and calmly. Let him think it out while you wait, holding out the new item for him to take as he drops the first. Say "Thank you!" as you pick up the dropped item, and hold it out for him to take again.

He'll soon learn that exchange is no robbery. When he appears with something in his mouth, you can extend your hand and ask (politely) to see it. Admire the item, reward him with a treat, and whenever possible give him back the item he gave you.

If your dog has already bitten while guarding something he values, you need to find a force-free trainer to work with straight away.

Associated complications

Further things that will often indicate a reactive dog (useful to observe when you have a puppy: reactivity often only shows itself during adolescence) are sensitivity to sound or touch, and separation anxiety.

Sound sensitivity

Very common in herding breeds, who are alert to the tiniest sound in the environment. Keep in mind that a dog's hearing is many times more sensitive than ours. Not only that, but they can hear things way out of our range.

There are plenty of dogs who come apart at the first firework. Once she knew what the sound meant, my Border Collie Tip would turn to jelly, tremble, and drool, as soon as she heard the "wheeeee" of a rocket going up. One of the benefits of her growing to the ripe old age of 15 meant that she had about three firework-free years as her hearing deteriorated with age!

You can work to desensitise your dog to the noise (more in a later chapter). Playing a sound recording at a volume so low that you can barely hear it is a good way to start. Gradually increase the volume as your dog shows she is still comfortable. I record firework displays on the tv at New Year and play them from time to time while we go about our normal business in the house. The sharp bangs and booms become an unremarkable experience.

Touch sensitivity

You'll find this in all sorts of dogs, notably in dogs who have been rescued. Touch has possibly become a bad thing for them. Street dogs may have had no experience of our touch in the critical socialisation and familiarisation period of very early puppyhood. Puppy farm (puppy mill) puppies will probably have had little touch stimulation from people. This as an experience all puppies should be introduced to early on.

A good way to do this is by counterconditioning and desensitisation (again - more in a later chapter). For now, use the Five Second Rule for touching a dog. If the dog wishes to interact with you, respond and touch, ruffle and chat, up to the count of five. Then move your hands, body, and face away. Your dog may want more, and nuzzle you to carry on your fussing. You can give another five seconds before pausing again. By the same token, if *you've* had enough, your dog should respect your turning away by stopping pestering you.

But your dog may surprise you, and give a quick shake and move away as soon as you stop. He's had enough! Quite revealing if it was your children doing the touching and counting. I'm not suggesting your children are doing bad things - just that your dog may be a bit wary of them and their unpredictability.

If your dog is over-sensitive to touch, be sure that any visitors know this routine. Known visitors should count up to only three seconds before releasing. Strangers, zero seconds.

An abnormally aggressive response to touch, especially in a sleeping dog, needs a thorough vet check for pain or other neurological cause.

Separation anxiety

It's been shown from studies that many dogs suffer a measure of anxiety when left alone. This can range from some discomfort all the way up to the mega-symptoms of endless howling, loss of bladder and bowel control, shredding anything they can get their teeth into - especially doors and doorframes - sometimes injuring themselves in their desperate attempts to escape.

Clearly, if your dog is showing these extreme symptoms, you need to deal with this straight away. Get help from a qualified force-free behaviourist, a veterinary behaviourist, or at the very least from a well-researched book (see Resources Section).

For lesser signs of agitation when you leave, start from puppyhood with crate-training or some other kind of barrier training. See the Resources Section for my book *Calm Down! Step-by-Step to a Calm, Relaxed, and Brilliant Family Dog*, the first book in the series **Essential Skills for a Brilliant Family Dog**.

Teach your pup how to relax at will, and be sure to give her things to chew while she nods off. Classical music (that's Mozart, Haydn and the like) has been proven to help dogs relax, so leave a suitable recording or radio station playing. A solid sleep routine is vital. And most importantly, practice leaving the pup for short periods right from the start, even if you stay in the house.

Not sure what your dog does when you're out? Leave a laptop or smartphone recording, then you'll know!

Even a small amount of separation anxiety is going to add up to a lot of stress for your dog. And to get the happy, carefree dog we all want means we have to eliminate as much stress as possible for him - in every part of his life.

Lack of impulse control

We all need impulse control. Your young child is able to leave the cakes on the table alone in the knowledge that he'll get some later on. Picture an adult with no impulse control. They're probably in jail.

Our dogs can learn impulse control just the same as we can. My dogs will leave those cakes on the table - even a nose-level coffee table - when I'm out of the room. This is a case of *what you expect is what you get.* I expect a lot of my dogs - but I do take the time to teach them first! They don't come with all this pre-installed.

For a detailed program to teach your dog impulse control, see the second book in the series **Essential Skills for a Brilliant Family Dog** - *Leave it! How to teach Amazing Impulse Control to your Brilliant Family Dog* (see Resources Section).

The skills involved will teach your dog to be reflective and thoughtful, instead of diving in gung-ho. These skills are essential to success in other parts of his life that he finds challenging.

ACTION STEP 1:

Acknowledge that it's not your dog's fault that she does what she does when out. You have a good dog - she just has problems in certain areas of her life. No need to blame her, her history, you, or anyone else. It just is.

But we're going to change it!

In this Chapter we have learnt that:

- Some dogs are more likely to be reactive than others
- They may be a victim of their heredity
- We need to treat the problem holistically
- Teaching calm and impulse control are essential
- Your dog needs help, not chiding

Section 2

Why did it start?

Chapter 3

The early days

Two pups meet freely on a Good for Dogs Puppy Walk

A lot of new puppy-owners are now aware of the importance of early socialisation. But many people think that it just means their puppy has to meet lots of dogs. While calm viewings and greetings and, where appropriate, play are indeed very important, there's a lot more to it than that. Socialisation, Familiarisation, and Habituation, should all go together.

That's to say, in their first 14 weeks of life puppies need to experience everything we expect them to live with in our world.

This will include dogs, cats, people, old people, children, washing machines, bikes, people arguing, cars, sheep, plastic sacks, waterways, hang-gliders, people with hats, dropped saucepans, stairs, shops, gravel paths, and so on. Everything they're going to encounter in normal life.

And while a lot of people have some idea that it's important, many of them sadly get it wrong, usually by leaving it far too late.

It should start with an excellent breeder who provides early enrichment in the puppies' environment, with objects, sounds, different textures, tastes, visitors, phones ringing, for example.

Even puppies with this good start can get lost along the way if fear of disease has them kept in the house till after 14 weeks. Fortunately more vets are understanding the importance of these early days, and recommend getting the pup out and about everywhere from Day 1 in your home – at about 8 weeks of age. (You can carry him.)

Socialisation and new experiences continue, of course, all the dog's life. The more novelty your dog encounters, the more he's likely to accept new things. These days dogs are kept indoors a lot more, separate from other dogs. In days gone by - and no doubt in some rural areas still - dogs were let out in the morning to wander where they wished. This is no longer safe or possible, and sadly we have lost a lot which contributed to the bombproof neighbourhood dogs of yesteryear.

As an example, I find that rescued street dogs tend to be great with other dogs, and afraid of people. This reflects their early life. They have learnt dog social skills and body language very well, which is why they survived. People perhaps represented danger.

Maturing, adolescence

Just like human teenagers, canine teenagers (approximately 6-14 months, depending on breed and size) go through a huge amount of hormone-driven change. They will get braver and venture further from their owner when out.

(This is also the time when your recall will break down, if you've just been relying on your puppy's infant clinginess to keep him coming back to you.) Some of this bravery may result in poor experiences. They may look almost full-grown, but the young dog's brain is still learning and changing.

One thing that can adversely affect this maturing process is early neutering - indeed neutering at any age can have undesired side-effects (see the Resources Section for info on the many scientific studies). By early I mean anything up to about 12 months.

We'll look at this in detail in Chapter 11. For now, hold off on the neutering plans.

Your dog's breed or type

We looked at the effect this can have on a tendency toward reactivity in Chapter 2, and found that guard breeds, guardian breeds, herding breeds, and terriers, were more likely to become reactive to novelty in their environment.

There's also a proclivity with some breeds to noise sensitivity and touch sensitivity. Anything that puts dogs into a heightened sense of awareness or adds stress to their lives is likely to erupt in the fear behaviour we've talked about.

Another aspect of this is that the friendly neighbourhood mutt that many of us grew up with — so suited to being a family pet - is being forced into extinction.

This is partly because of the aggressive neutering policies espoused by some cultures. The friendly neighbourhood breeding stock has been wiped out.

And the rise in consumerism has spilled over into dog ownership too, with its emphasis on having the latest, the best, the most fashionable - of everything.

It would make no sense for me to get a performance sports car: I drive at reasonable speeds, and need lots of space to carry family, dogs, and all their gear.

By the same token, it's not appropriate for many normal family households to take in a high-performance dog, which for generations has been bred for - tramping the moors eight hours a day; hurtling over or through any obstacles in their path to fetch and drive sheep; hunting down and killing anything small and furry; or patrolling properties all night on the lookout for ne'er-do-wells and intruders.

This is a placing which is not going to work!

Choosing a dog by its looks alone, without considering the purpose which has produced those looks, as well as the dog's needs and energy and stamina levels, is doomed to disappointment.

In this chapter we have learnt that:

- Outside factors can affect a dog's likelihood to become reactive
- It's possible to minimise these effects
- Choose "horses for courses"

Chapter 4

Medical causes

Clearly, a medical condition can affect your dog's character. There could be hidden pain that will naturally be stressful, tiring, and would put anyone on a short fuse!

I am not a vet, but I'm aware that there are also conditions which have been shown to affect a dog's worldview.

ACTION STEP 2:

Before embarking on any program of training or behaviour modification, you need to establish that your dog is sound. It's possible that some kind of medication will make a big difference, mentally or physically. So a thorough vet check (not just a quick once-over) is indicated. If you know your dog is experiencing pain or lameness, you can have a session with a qualified canine massage therapist, who are very good at uncovering slight or intermittent sensitivities. (This isn't snake-oil - it's a proper, recognised qualification!)

Personal history

Your dog may have been fine with other dogs up until the day he was attacked, let's say by a black terrier. Now he is (with some justification) afraid of all terriers, or all black dogs, or all male dogs, or all dogs.

Maybe your dog came from a shelter. You may know his previous history or you may not. Clearly it was not good, or he wouldn't have ended up in the shelter. Even if he was much loved by someone who has died, this is a scarring experience. For some dogs, a shelter is a 24/7 nightmare. I'm not blaming the hardworking and dedicated shelter staff here: for me, being transported to a holiday camp would be a nightmare!

Maybe the staff say he was "fine" with other dogs. Maybe he was. Maybe he was shut down and "keeping a low profile" (as I would, at that holiday camp!). The true dog was not apparent. It can take a dog at least eight weeks to settle into a new home and feel fully relaxed there.

If you went to live in someone else's home, you would start off being super-polite and considerate. "Where does this cup go?" "Is it alright if I sit here?" and such like. But after a few weeks, you'd be leaving cups on the floor, putting your feet on the furniture, and generally making yourself feel at home. So it is with your dog. Once he's truly relaxed and knows he belongs (that's a good thing!) he'll start to show sides of his character you didn't know existed (and that's fun!).

Copycats

If you are already blessed with a reactive dog, and you introduce a new dog into your household, take care not to take them out together until you're sure that your new dog is ok in the outside world. This reactivity is highly catching! And you may find you have not just two dogs barking (even if one's only doing it for the hell of it) but one may "redirect" a bite onto the other. Or you. That means because they can't reach the dog or person they want to frighten off, they grab the nearest thing, which could be your hand or thigh.

> ACTION STEP 3:
>
> If you get a new dog or puppy, rear it largely separately from your other dog. This is normal good practice in order to prevent your new pup becoming totally dog-focussed, and to give your older dog a break. If your older dog is reactive, then no group walks until your puppy is maybe a year old.

Fence running and window barking

Fence running (racing up and down inside your fence, barking at passing dogs, or the dog next door) and window barking (perching inside the window and alerting to anything that moves) are bad habits you don't want any dog getting into.

But for the reactive dog it's even worse. Being on guard duty all day long when he should be resting and sleeping is exhausting. And all this guarding behind a safe barrier gives a false confidence - a kind of Dutch courage from the heady repetition. When this dog is out and sees a dog, he thinks "Gulp! This one's not behind a fence or a window - now I'm in trouble!" and lets loose with his full panoply of barking, lunging and terrorising.

Remedies for window barking can be found in the free e-course at www.brilliantfamilydog.com For fence running you can employ similar strategies, only outside. The first of these is never leave your dog alone in the garden or yard.

If you don't want something to happen, you must make sure it can't happen.

In this chapter we have learnt that

- There may be hidden causes for your dog's behaviour
- You must ensure your dog is in the full of his health
- There are four things that can make it all worse!

Section 3

Why did it get worse, when I'm trying my best?

Chapter 5

It will get worse - unless dealt with

There are some things that dogs do that will go away on their own. Some puppy behaviours, like chewing, submission-weeing, digging, will simply evaporate if carefully managed. But there are other things - usually the things we really don't want! - that will build and build, getting worse and worse, until we decide to do something about it.

When we do something for the first time, a neural pathway in the brain is built. To begin with this pathway is fairly narrow and hard to find. Think, learning to drive a car - it's all foreign to us and hard to remember the sequences. But the more we repeat that thing, the wider and brighter the neural pathway becomes until we can just slide down it without a thought. It becomes our go-to response. We can drive on auto-pilot!

So every time your dog does something, he's building those neural pathways bigger and stronger. He doesn't have to think hard, as the learner-driver would to locate which pedal to press. It becomes his automatic, instant, response. In the case of our reactive dog: "See dog: bark!"

While this all started as a fear response, it's now become a habit as well. So while we change the fear response, we will also be teaching new and better habits.

It works for the dog

If there's something that's frightening you, your first instinct is to get away from it. If you can't get away from *it*, you'll try to get *it* away from *you*. Hence some manic responses to a wasp in the house!

When your dog puts on a song and dance routine of barking, whining, lunging, and prancing, at the sight of another dog, he's trying to get it to go away.

And this often works!

Either

- the other dog is frightened off and moves away
- the other dog's owner thinks "this is a nasty dog" and turns away, OR
- the barking dog's owner is shamed into beating a hasty retreat

If it works, he'll keep doing it. *Because he has no other course of action to rely on.*

Fight or flight

This well-known expression really comes into its own with the reactive dog. It's the reason many people think their dog is "fine" off-lead, but turns into a monster on-lead. As we saw in Chapter 1, this dog is usually not as "fine" as people think. It's only because the off-lead dog has the freedom to move away (*flight*) that things don't go badly wrong.

Once your dog is tethered to you, however, he knows he can't flee, so this leaves only *fight*. This can all be made worse by the fact that he's unable to express his body language and calming signals. It's difficult to look nonchalant and relaxed if your head is being held up in the air.

Trapped in a tunnel!

This feeling of being restrained or trapped can also be made worse by being in a "tunnel". This is the stuff of nightmares for many people: ahead is an all-consuming fire, behind is a crush of people and cars - panic!

For your dog this tunnel could be made up of walls and hedges and parked cars, as on a street pavement, or can be a real tunnel of a narrow footpath with walls and trees either side. Even being 10 yards from a field barrier - trees, or a hedge - can prompt the *fight* reflex, as the *flight* option is limited.

And what does the owner bring to this party?

Sadly, we often make this all far, far worse.

I know we don't want to, and we think we're doing everything we can to stop it. But we do tend to add fuel to the fire.

If you're like 99% of reactive dog owners, you'll be in a continuous state of shock and apprehension when out with your dog - just waiting for something to kick off. So you wind the lead round your hand a few times, just to be sure, to be sure. You keep your dog on a tight lead, close to you - as if creeping through enemy territory and waiting for mines to start exploding any moment.

And the second you spot another dog - BANG! Off goes the first mine. You gasp and breathe in sharply, you go trembly and flustery, you tighten that lead even further, gripping it to your chest. "Oh no!" says your dog, "What's she so afraid of? What have I got to bark at?"

Your understandable fear and anxiety over your dog is now triggering your dog's outburst.

A loose cannon

It may be that, up to now, you've really had little understanding of *why* your dog behaves as she does. You know all too well *how* she behaves! It seems to you that she is unpredictable. She's lovely at home, so why does she put on this other persona when out?

You've come to distrust your friend.

And this feeling of unease, distrust, panic, seeps into even the calmest of walks. Your dog is now on her toes! If *you're* afraid, then there must be something bad out there. Your dog will work hard to locate it and try and keep it away.

How stressful a pleasant walk with your dog has become!

This is no fun for either of you, and this is what we are going to change. But wait, there's more you need to know first.

A social pariah

Maybe you've found that the only way out of this nightmare is to walk your dog at 5 in the morning, or at dead of night - at The Hour of the Difficult Dog. The only people you see are other owners of difficult dogs, who will scurry away like rats in the sunlight as soon as they spot you.

You have now become a social pariah. When you first got your dog, you had happy visions of companionable walks with friends and their dogs. What has happened? Walks have now become a chore. There's no fun here for either you or your dog.

You know that what you've been doing up to now is not working. So here's a complete turnaround for you - and you'll be quite amazed at the difference it will make!

> ACTION STEP 4
>
> As soon as you spot another dog,
>
> 1. Relax
> 2. Soften your hands on the lead, keeping it loose
> 3. Breathe out
> 4. Say cheerily to your dog, "Let's go!" while you turn and head the other direction.

I can hear your protests already! Just try it. We'll address problems and fallout later.

In this chapter we have learnt

- That hoping it will all go away will not work
- Why your dog is choosing this response
- Where instinct comes into it
- How we are unwittingly exacerbating the situation
- How a change in your mindset can make a big difference to your dog

Chapter 6

Previous training

If your dog came to you as a re-home, you'll have had no input into his previous training. But if you've owned your dog from a puppy, you are responsible for any previous training your dog has had.

Though maybe not entirely.

- You may have gone to your local dog training school in the hope of giving your puppy the very best start in life
- You could have followed a tv personality who everyone is talking about
- Perhaps you took the advice of other dogwalkers or family members

Sadly, you may have found the only training offered to you was aversive training. The type of punishment-based training that used to be meted out to children in days (happily) gone by. You may have found these ideas run contrary to how you like to bring up your children, or deal with co-workers, but you were assured that these teachers knew best and that it was different with animals, so you went along with it.

What damage may have been done!

Any kind of aversive training can have a devastating effect on a dog's confidence in his ability to cope, or show emotions. If a dog has been punished when he saw a dog approaching and was afraid of it, how's he now going to feel about approaching dogs? "CLEAR OFF before I get into trouble!" is his noisy answer.

If that punishment has been with the gruesomely mediaeval prong collar, a painful choke chain, or for true barbarism, an electric shock collar, his response is going to be stronger and faster.

You will have to work against a fear reaction born of real pain. I hope I don't need to tell you to ditch any of this equipment if it's in your house? We'll be looking at humane equipment later on.

But don't blame yourself. You did the best you could with the knowledge you had. We're starting with a clean slate now, so there's no time for regrets or "what if's".

Punishment tends to drive problems underground. The hungry child who is beaten for stealing will not stop stealing: he'll just make sure he's never caught again! His hunger and deprivation won't go away. In the same way, if you punish an emotional response in a dog you aren't addressing the problem, just suppressing the reaction. The problem is still very much there, but with lots more anxiety attached to it. "I was afraid of the other dog - now I'm afraid of my owner too!" is not going to help change your dog's state of mind.

And suppressed emotions can get bottled up until, one day, the cork is blown out of the bottle and everything comes out, in a massive over-reaction!

Many dogs find themselves punished for growling, for example.

Never punish a dog for growling!

"Punishing a dog for growling is like taking the batteries out of a smoke alarm." Very well put by dog trainer Nando Brown. If your dog is not allowed to tell you of his anxiety by a low rumble of discomfort, then he may skip that step and go straight to the next one up - snapping or biting.

Regard growling as information. Your dog is telling you something – that he is really not happy with the situation. So you need either to remove him from the pressure, or remove the pressure from him.

Punishment can have a lot of unintended fallout. Punishment may involve pain and fear. But it may be much milder - like forcing a frightened dog to be in a place with lots of screaming children. You may not have intended to punish that dog, but that's what happened, in effect. And the erosion of the dog's trust in you, as well as your evident annoyance, is burying that problem ever deeper in the dog's mind.

If you get fish-poisoning after a restaurant meal, not only are you never going to that restaurant again - maybe you'll never eat fish again! A rather extreme response to a single event. But understandable.

Stress

And while we're looking at making things worse, we cannot overlook stress. Stress causes reactions to be exaggerated. Stress causes us to snap. Likewise your dog. And there are some areas of your dog's life that are building stress that will really surprise you.

1. Too many walks

"What!" you squawk! "I thought I had to take my dog out for a walk every single day! I thought I was doing the right thing!" Well, like so much in life, that depends. It depends on how your dog is experiencing these walks. A happy-go-lucky dog who loves meeting people and other dogs will relish his daily walks. But that's not the dog you have, or you wouldn't be reading this book.

It may be that your dog gets sick with anxiety at the very thought of a walk. The walk may consist of you getting upset or telling him off while he runs the gauntlet of narrow paths, fence-running dogs, squealing children, dog walkers walking their dog straight towards him, traffic noises, people wanting to pat his head …

This is not an enjoyable walk for an anxious, shy, or reactive dog!

There are two reasons for walking your dog. One is for exercise. The other is for socialisation. Clearly the second reason is a fail. So cut your losses, exercise your dog with vigorous play in the garden or on solo walks in a relatively dog-free zone - a forest trail, for instance - and save road walks for when your dog is calm and you can avoid most of the hazards.

We're focussing on the outcome here, guys - Calm walks with a happy and relaxed dog. If your daily walks are not a step in this direction, then you need to cut them right back.

2. Not enough sleep

Meggie and Marty hard at work

This one floors so many people! Adult dogs need to sleep 17 hours a day for mental and physical stability. 17 hours a day! Is your dog getting anywhere near 17 hours a day? If your dog paces and runs, chews and barks, jumps and dives, plays and chases all the time at home, he is not living the carefree life you may imagine! I have seen the dramatic improvements that result from getting this one right.

Teaching your dog how to relax, switch off, and get that urgently-needed restorative sleep will transform your dog's worldview. For a full guided program, check out *Calm Down! Step-by-step to a Calm, Relaxed and Brilliant Family Dog,* the first book in the series **Essential Skills for a Brilliant Family Dog.** It's free at all e-book stores, and you can find the details in the Resources Section.

Yawn …

3. Stress in the home

Your home may be a wonderful, sunny, joyful place of love and harmony. But your dog can still get stressed there! There may be anxiety when she's left alone. There could be rumbling disagreements with another family pet. The new puppy is driving her nuts and won't leave her alone. There could be so much noise and activity from the children and their school friends, that your dog can't get a moment's peace. Maybe you have a thieving problem with your dog which causes some friction. Perhaps she barks at the window, annoyingly.

Solutions to these problems can be found referenced in the Resources Section. The thieving, for instance, can be resolved, painlessly, by the second book in the series **Essential Skills for a Brilliant Family Dog**: *Leave it! How to teach Amazing Impulse Control to your Brilliant Family Dog.* And you'll find a free e-course for all those annoying habits your darling dog has developed.

4. Daycare or a dogwalker

A very perceptive reader sent me this query recently: "My question is, what do you think of daycare for dogs? Are the dogs actually happy about it, or do dog owners just like to imagine they are?"

I am not going to tar all daycares and dogwalkers with the same brush. But I will say that it's very hard to find a convenient one which is truly a safe place for your dog to learn and develop. Think of the skills you need as a parent to prevent open warfare in your own household! Then picture a gang of dogs being thrown together for a walk - or all day in a confined area - in the care of people who frequently have no dog training or behaviour qualifications whatever. "I love dogs" may help, but it's not a qualification. And given how long it takes us to learn how to care for our own species - and that a lot of what people think about dogs is wrong - you're going to be lucky to find somewhere safe for your dog.

I was recently shown a promotional video for a daycare by someone who's been sending her very reactive German Shepherd pup there for months. Even in this 30-second video - meant to show how wonderful the place was - I could see bullying and intimidation of this pup by other dogs, and no-one going to her aid. Imagine what this sensitive puppy is subjected to for ten hours a day, five days a week! No wonder her reactivity is already extreme at only six months of age. What the owner thought as "being perfectly happy at daycare" was in fact a dog that spent all day trying to avoid the other dogs (quite impossible with those numbers of loose dogs) - shut down, in other words. Not fine at all.

For many dogs, daycare is viewed with the same suspicion I view that holiday camp!

My personal solution to an enforced absence from home is to have someone I trust to come in to let the dogs out in the garden and play with them for a while during the day.

If anything goes wrong in a daycare or with a dogwalker, you will be paying for that for years - possibly the rest of your dog's life. Think hard, and do a lot of homework, before going for that option. Apart from checking out the daycare's mission statement for aversive practices, you could do well by asking to spend an hour just observing, or join the dogwalker for one of her walks.

In this chapter we've learnt that

- Old sins have long shadows
- Stress, the silent killer, can affect your dog even when you think you are doing the best for her

Chapter 7

Other factors that can make things worse

Diet

I am not a vet.

We all know how much diet affects our health, and we take care to ensure we're following government guidelines, and to minimise the junk our children get hold of. We also know the value of a varied diet of fresh foods, so that we get the greatest spread of nutrients.

So why do people chuck that all out of the window when feeding their dog?

Their dog has to put up with the same bag of food - often with a ridiculously long shelf life and sell-by date - year in, year out. No variation, no broad spread of nutrients, no fun.

Commercial dog food is big business! But sadly, choosing the bag with the cutest picture is not the way to get the best for your dog. A little online research will take you to a comparison site for dog foods for your part of the world. Look for a site written by a canine nutritionist, rather than a manufacturer. And take care that it is independent and in no way affiliated with the manufacturers it's putting at the top of the charts.

Clearly, what affects the body also affects the mind. You can't feel ready to face the world if your skin is poor or your joints aching. So the reactive dog needs special care in regard to food.

Here are some pointers for you:

1. If it's advertised widely and available in prime position at your local supermarket, you should probably avoid it.

2. If its first ingredients feature cereals (maize, corn, wheat, barley) you should definitely avoid it. Dogs are not chickens.

3. If it has named protein sources (e.g. lamb, beef, not "meat"), no chemical additives, and you can't see the word "derivative" in the list, it's probably a good bet.

4. Many people consider a raw diet of meaty bones, offal, fish, and egg, as the most suitable diet for a dog. You can get this in convenient frozen packs, but be sure to augment with fresh stuff from your local butcher.

5. Your dog's poo should be firm and small. Copious loose stools (in an otherwise healthy dog) can be an indicator of a poor diet, as the dog is not absorbing his food but sending it all straight through.

6. Commercial dog treats can be very poor quality. Make your own fresh ones! Very easy, and cheaper - I'll be covering that in these books.

7. Whatever you choose to feed, ring the changes! If you and I ate the exact same diet, one of us may get fat and be short of, say, iron, while the other may get thin and have an excess of iron. (You can tell I'm not a doctor either!) We are individuals.

You have to become a good stockman and feed for condition. Ignore the feeding quantities written on the pack, and keep a close eye or hand on your dog's body condition. You should be able to feel the ribs, but not cut yourself on them! You should be able to easily locate the pin bones at the top of the pelvis, and there should be no hard rolls of fat round the neck and shoulders. Your dog's walking should be smooth and fluent, not a swaying waddle.

Feeding the best diet you can afford for your dog (and the best feeds are by no means necessarily the most expensive) will save you a boatload of money in non-attendance at the vet. Your dog's teeth will be white and naturally clean, his skin and coat good, his joints well held together, his health at optimum level. That is what I have found in my own dogs.

> ## ACTION STEP 5:
>
> Check out dog foods (don't die of shock when you read the label on the one you're feeding!) and move your dog up to a better one. Some change in behaviour can often be seen in as little as two weeks. Change the food gradually over a few days to allow the gut to catch up to the new food.

Copying your other dog

As mentioned in Chapter 4, copying your older reactive dog can be disastrous. The two dogs give each other Dutch courage. And barking is very self-rewarding - fun!

So if you're struggling to walk the two of them together, make life easier for yourself and walk them separately most of the time. You may, for instance, take Dog A out for a roadwalk on-lead one morning, and Dog B the next. They can have joint walks when it's mostly free running, perhaps each day. But refer back to **Chapter 6: Stress** and be sure your fearful or anxious dog is not getting too many bad experiences on walks.

Solo walks give you time to enjoy each dog separately, and if your walks have been a battle wrestling with twisting leads and spinning, barking dogs, they'll restore the pleasure to your walks. Sometimes your reactive dog gets the lion's share of attention, so taking your calmer dog on walks alone with you is very valuable to build that bond. Remember, your younger dog can become very dependent on your older dog if they spend too much time together - with catastrophic results when you lose the older dog. It's important to foster an independent spirit in your younger dog.

Other owners

This is where things can get tricky and unpredictable. Being told you have a nasty dog when you are trying to untangle the lead from your legs and calm said dog down is less than helpful. Having another dog owner stand in front of you being snooty about their dog's good behaviour is *no help at all* when your dog is reacting to their proximity!

We feel a lot of social pressure to put up with things we don't like and not rock the boat. In this case you are your dog's sole protector. If you know your dog needs distance, then that's what you give her.

Don't mind what other people think. You may never see them again, and what do they know? If their dog is calm around other dogs, they have *no idea* what we have to cope with! I once heard someone on the radio, referencing the straitened circumstances of her early adult life, saying something like: "Nobody who has money and no children can know what it's like to have children and no money."

And I'll add that nobody who has a dog who can handle every situation can know what it's like to have a dog who is frightened of almost everything.

Know that - once you've absorbed all the precepts in this book - you are doing your best for your anxious dog, and you'll know by seeing the great changes that will take place. Don't worry about the know-it-alls!

.. and other dogs

There's always going to be a time when you have to cope with an incoming dog. And whether it's over-friendly or aggressive, it will have a similar effect on your dog.

There are various suggestions for what you can do. Some people, knowing that their dog is better off-lead - and obviously only if there's no road nearby - will unclip the lead and keep back, ready to call their dog out for a treat or toy if things are going downhill. Others suggest tossing a handful of treats towards the incomer.

I know that asking the owner to call their dog is a total waste of time. Why? Because they have zero recall and they're not about to demonstrate that to you!

Sometimes I've caught the incoming dog by the collar and waited for the owner to trudge the 100 yards or so to come and fetch him. You need to be feeling strong enough to face their ire if you try this. If your dog is very small, you can teach her to jump up into your arms. Her jumping up is safer than you bending down and putting your face between the incomer and your dog. If the dog is going to grab your dog, they may grab you too.

You can try turning and running away, but dogs run very fast! Whatever you do, don't use any kind of aversive gadget (like a spray or noise), which will affect your dog just as much as the other dog, and make things much worse next time it happens.

Fortunately, in my own experience, genuine dog-dog attacks are pretty rare. Usually it's all sound and fury signifying nothing. The dogs have good bite inhibition, in other words. Real, savage, attacks can happen as a result of a misplaced strong predatory drive, and for that reason I keep my small fluffy dog still or lifted up when blooded greyhounds are in the vicinity.

Later on, you'll be learning an Emergency Turn which is tremendously useful for getting your reactive dog to forget the incomer and bounce away with you. This normally causes the other dog's advance to fizzle out. I'll also be giving you lots of advice on coping with an incoming dog. Real help is on the way in the next book! But learning first what's going on and why things are happening is critical to your future success in changing your life.

In the next Section we are going to learn some key skills and strategies to get you going in the right direction. Towards calm, peaceful walks.

In this chapter, we have learnt that:

- What you're putting into your dog's mouth can greatly affect his mindset
- Other family dogs can make things worse
- Other people and their dogs can make things a lot worse!

Section 4

What can I do?

Chapter 8

Change

"NOW you're talking!"

We've taken a good look at what is up with our dog, what started it, and what made it worse and kept it going. Now we're going to look at what we can do about it.

The first thing is to change. Obviously, you want things to change. But a lot of this change is going to come from *you*. Without change we can't expect different results. They say that it's a sign of madness to keep doing the same thing and expect a different result!

You see it every day when someone in the park calls their dog - to whom they have not taught a recall. They stand and yell. And yell. And YELL. They get crosser and crosser and their dog still doesn't come. They need to change something or they can stand there all day calling. (Hint: if he won't come to you, go to him. And cut the yelling.)

So we need to change our mindset. This was hinted at in the Action Step for Chapter 2: *Acknowledge that it's not your dog's fault*. It's so easy to blame someone or something when things go wrong. Blame is counterproductive. It just gives people an outlet for their frustration without doing anything material to effect a change. I'm not suggesting you blame yourself either, though as you saw in Chapter 5, you most probably contributed to it.

So many times people say "Ah well, he's a rescue dog ..." and this after having had the dog for five years! He may once have been a rescue dog, but after a rescue dog has been in my home for a few minutes he's now *my* dog, no longer a "rescue dog". Parents don't say, "These are our children, but that one's adopted." You'd be scandalised! Accept that this dog is now your dog, that what went before is out of your control, and that moving forward together things will change for the better. No need to wind back the clock and try and blame something that happened long ago. Start from where you are.

As you learn new ways to work with your reactive dog you'll grow in confidence and understanding. You'll begin to truly empathise with your dog. You'll understand her. And she'll love that and respond to it. You're in it together.

The training method that works

Whatever system, method, or vague idea you were working with before, you are now going to switch over to choice-based training. Why? Because it works! But seriously, it's been scientifically proven to work. That is to say there have been many experimental studies, using scientifically approved methods for testing parameters and data collection, which prove beyond doubt that it works. There isn't any argument.

There are still plenty of people, sadly, who don't hold with this science nonsense and think that bullying and intimidation is a better method. But we'll leave them to stew in their own juice while we move forward into the light and do the job properly.

I'm not going off on a rant about the horrors of punishment-based training. If you've come this far with me, you probably share a lot of my views already. Suffice to say that if you put yourself into the position of the dog who is being poked, shouted at, threatened, given electric shocks, swung in the air by the throat till they are suffocating (all established "training" techniques) you would not be feeling very well disposed to the world in general. Miserable, in fact. And ready to bite the next thing that comes near you.

So what is choice-based training?

This simply means that you accord your dog a measure of intelligence and autonomy, and involve him in decisions which affect him.

So instead of saying, "Do this," you'll be saying, "What should you do now?" And no, this is not a recipe for chaos. You teach your dog to think, to problem-solve, to work out what is the best action to take at any given time. Now, instead of having a dog you bark "commands" at and who largely disregards them ("Sit, stay, SIT, I said sit, come here, stay, sit, WILL you come here, stay, good boy, sit!" Sounds familiar? It's exactly what I heard someone saying to their dog this morning), you have a dog who anticipates the right action and offers a sit when it seems a good idea, and then stays sitting until released.

You build this up by the simple method of:

Reward what you like
Ignore what you don't like
Manage what you can't ignore

This is now your mantra! Recite it daily, and twice before breakfast.

Until you get going with some of the Action Steps coming, where the speed of learning may surprise you, you'll just have to believe me when I say that it's that simple! You'll have an engaged and active learner, you'll be doing nothing remotely nasty, and your dog will build an ever stronger bond with you.

I discovered early in my parenting career that framing things as a positive removed huge amounts of conflict from my day. So we had:

Not "No boots in the house"
but "Boots go outside"

Not "Don't come to the table in pyjamas"
but "Boys who are dressed get breakfast"

Not "No tv till you've done your homework"
but "Would you like to watch your programme then do homework, or homework first?"
(There was no offer of skipping homework.)

Not "No computer games"
but "Do twenty minutes typing training then you get to play twenty minutes games"

This one really paid off as both boys could touch-type very fast by age 12 - one of my early goals for them.

Honour the dog

This goes hand in hand with acknowledging that it's not your dog's fault. He has opinions and feelings himself, and by honouring those feelings you can show true empathy. Your dog is not an automaton, a toy for people to play with. He's a sentient being and has a right to be consulted, and his thoughts and feelings taken into account.

Your dog is not something you do things to. *He's someone you do things* with.

Diet

If you want an engine to function properly, you have to put in the right fuel. We know this for our car. We also know this for our family. Extend this to your dog! If you haven't already done so, follow Action Step 5 in Chapter 7 -

to thoroughly research feeding options for your dog, and make the necessary improvements.

Understanding

I hope that by now, having read the first part of this book, that you have a far greater understanding of what is going on with your dog. Knowing that he's not a bad dog, just a frightened one, will make a difference to how you manage him when out.

You can cope far better with the social pressures that afflict you when your dog is on his toes, ready to erupt at a passer-by, when you know that he's a good dog having difficulty. Dogs are not people, and we need to understand how the mind of another species works. I find that the more I learn about my dogs, the closer our bond becomes, and the more I marvel at the fact that the human race can live so harmoniously and mutually beneficially with another species. It is truly an honour to experience this.

I will be telling you a lot about how dogs think and do. You'll find this an area of continuing interest - the more you learn, the more you'll want to learn! Having said that, you do not have to be a scientist or a professional dog trainer to make the techniques work. You do need a measure of understanding - especially of the fallout of doing things the wrong way - so you can field all those "helpful suggestions" volunteered by people who have no expertise, and put them in the "Thank you, I'll bear that in mind" folder. (Then never open that folder again.)

Take pressure off the dog

Your first priority is always going to be to keep your dog calm. "Under threshold" as it's sometimes known - the threshold being the doorway from calm to lunatic. "What about keeping *me* calm?" you say! See this: if your dog is calm, you will be calm.

And yes! it can happen. Not only *can* it happen, but it *will* happen. You may have been promised the earth by a previous trainer, who used old-fashioned methods to intimidate the dog into different behaviour. Quite often, the dog behaves very well with that trainer, then reverts to type with you - because you're not prepared to pursue the methods used and inflict pain and suffering on your dog.

The methods I will be showing you are all entirely force-free, and involve the dog making good decisions. This is what will effect a genuine change in your dog - it's not inflicted from without, but grows from within.

You will have the pure joy of looking into your dog's eyes when a situation arises that would previously have sent him into a tailspin - and seeing reflected there the calm confidence you feel, and the appreciation he feels for you.

Your dog needs a stress-free zone to learn new ways of reacting before applying them in a stimulating situation. So your first change is going to be in where you take your dog.

You may have been advised to keep exposing your dog to her fears, either in the name of socialisation or as a training technique. As we saw earlier, true Socialisation only takes place between the ages of 3-14 weeks.

But experiencing new things should always involve good experiences, and the dog should be taken away from anything that she's not happy about. Imagine you were terrified of mice: would it help you to have to put your hand into a cage full of them? As they crawled over your arm and nibbled your fingernails, would this make you less afraid of them? Would it perhaps make you anxious about the "expert" who was making you do this? This technique is known as "flooding" and is discredited as a humane method of working with a dog. We'll look at this in more detail in Book 3, Chapter 1.

So the dog that's afraid of traffic is *not* forced to stand at a busy crossroads for an hour (yes, people do this). This way you'll end up with a dog that's more afraid of traffic than before! Now I'm sure you want to minimise the stress your dog is under, and not force him to tolerate situations which are frightening for him.

Having to spend hours in the close and inescapable proximity of other dogs, whether in a daycare or group dogwalking setup, group classes, or on walks in narrow confined spaces, such as streets and footpaths, is stressful for someone who fears dogs! So this is where you're going to make some changes.

I know some may be hard to implement. You may have to pay slightly more for a more personal dog-sitting service; you may have to get the car out and drive to suitable walk spaces; you may be sorry to have to leave the group classes that *you* enjoy. But our aim is at this stage to focus on your dog's wellbeing and state of mind. Nothing will change until we change that.

ACTION STEP 6:

Check out alternatives to daycare. Either a very small family group in a private home, or a minder who can visit during your absence. Your fearful dog does not need to be taken for a walk by someone else - especially someone who doesn't know this stuff.

ACTION STEP 7:

Change or quit training class. Classes should have no more than eight puppies or six dogs. They should be calm, and focussed on the individual dog and owner. No shouting. No punishment. No threatening or intimidation. The trainer should be professionally qualified and part of a force-free organisation (see Resources Section).

ACTION STEP 8:

First of all, if walks are miserable and tense, cut down the walks! Exercise your dog at home and venture out only to places which are safe for him. Seek out open spaces where you can see incomers for hundreds of yards all around you. Avoid narrow paths and "tunnels", and anything that makes your dog feel trapped.

ACTION STEP 9:

This step is critical! *Show your dog she never has to meet another dog or person ever again.* When you and your dog see something coming that you know will upset her, you say a cheery "Let's go!", turn, and head in another direction. Your reward will be the relief you see in her face.

In this chapter we have looked at some of the changes you will have to make:

- Your attitude to your dog and her problem
- Seeking out and understanding a new training approach
- Understanding your dog and empathising with her
- Changing some of your habits and current practices
- Avoidance

Chapter 9 Keep changing!

The Precious Name Game

Your dog's name should be precious. She should think that it always means something good - she should be in no doubt about that. If you've ever spoken to your dog in frustration (hands up, guys - which of us hasn't lost it on occasion?) as in "Flossie? Who did this?" or "Flossie-get-over-here-this-instant!", then you've set up a bit of conflict in your dog's mind about whether "Flossie" means undiluted fun and pleasure or an impending telling-off.

So you need to make a change here straight away! The answer is simple. You only use your dog's name when you can pair it with good things. And if you're ever frustrated or annoyed, you don't use her name. Watch out for other family members as well as yourself. You may be surprised at how much negativity is being attached to your dog's name on a daily basis!

Lesson 1
The Precious Name Game

Here's a simple game to get you started - the Precious Name Game:

- Say dog's name cheerily whenever you notice her
- When she responds - by raising an eyebrow or hurtling towards you and crashing into your legs - reward her with something good
- Repeat at every opportunity throughout the day
- Enjoy your dog

Your reward may be a treat, putting her lead on for a walk (if walks are enjoyable), opening the door to the garden, playing a game, and so on. We'll look at rewards in greater depth in the next book.

Collar hold

This is - maybe surprisingly - another relationship-builder. If your dog stands still for you to slip your hand in her collar, this indicates a measure of trust - especially if it's in a tricky situation where she's worried.

If your dog is young and playful, she may intercept an approaching hand with her mouth, in order to start a game. Not so good. And if your dog has recently been re-homed with you there may be a history of collar-grabbing, dragging, and hurting (remember, we're not going to go there and use it as an excuse) which makes her understandably uneasy about having her collar felt.

So we're going to teach anew that your hand in your dog's collar means only good things. You'll see it's similar to the Precious Name Game above.

Lesson 2
The Collar Hold

Here's how you do it:

1. Have a supply of scrummy treats to hand
2. Have one treat ready in one hand, and with the other hand reach out and touch the side of your dog's face - just for a second - then remove your hand, feed the treat
3. Repeat Step 2 until she's happy to let you touch her face
4. Repeat Step 2, but reach and touch the side of her neck - just for a second - then remove your hand, feed the treat
5. Repeat Step 4 till she's happy
6. Repeat Step 4, but touch the collar for a second before feeding the

treat

7. Keep going till you can slip a finger into her collar, remove your hand - feed treat

8. Eventually you'll be able to slide your hand softly into her collar, with the back of your hand resting against her neck, and walk a few steps with her beside you before feeding the treat

9. When you reach towards your dog's collar she'll stay still and allow you to hold it then stay with you

Watchpoints:

- This will take as long as it takes. Maybe one session of a couple of minutes, maybe ten sessions - doesn't matter

- Be sure to remove your touching hand before feeding the treat

- Work very fast - touch-remove-treat, touch-remove-treat, keep it light and fun

- You are never pulling on this collar, not even gripping it firmly

- The goal is to be able to slip your hand into your dog's collar whenever you need to

When your dog feels the back of your hand against her neck she will now relax and stay still beside you. This is a great calming strategy for a reactive or anxious dog.

ACTION STEP 10:

Practice both these new skills daily. Little and often, and only in a safe place where your dog is relaxed and comfortable (most of my training takes place spontaneously, for just a minute or two, in the kitchen). The very thought of these games should produce a happy tail-wag.

Lead Skills

"Lead skills? You just clip the lead on the dog and hang on tight, don't you?" If that's what you're thinking, even a little, I am about to open up a new world for you! A world where you communicate with your dog, give her confidence and courage, and allow her to be a dog - all through your lead. And as a spin-off, your shoulders will stay comfortable, and your walks more relaxed.

The key thing here is that once you've mastered these skills, *you will never have to pull your dog's lead again.* What joy!

With a reactive and unpredictable dog, you've probably been holding on pretty tight to that lead. You've maybe thought that you have to have close control the whole time or else your dog will cut loose and savage someone. I really do understand! I've been there myself.

But you'll be pleased to know that in fact the opposite is true. The more relaxed your hands are on the lead, the more relaxed your dog will be. You want to change your mindset from desperate control, to protecting and helping your dog.

The lead is there to keep your dog from running under a bus, and to help with her self-control when she sees something that worries her, and, most importantly, it's a connection between the two of you. Messages go up and down this lead. Keeping it tight with a vice-like grip will prevent any communication.

The Opposition Reflex

If you were standing next to me and I pulled your arm - you'd pull back. You have to, in order to stay upright. This is called the Opposition Reflex and stops us falling over all the time.

Your dog has the same reflex! So if you pull his collar, he's going to pull away from you, in order to stay upright. If your lead is really tight - so tight that your dog is straining into his collar and your hands and arms are aching as you pull back - and I come along with a pair of scissors and cut the lead in half, what's going to happen? You'll probably both fall over!

So let's stop this madness now and make life easier for both of you.

It takes two to tango, as the saying goes, and it takes two to have a tight lead.

One of us has to stop pulling, and as we're the ones with the bigger brains, it needs to be us. Sadly, this pulling has often started in puppyhood and is now an entrenched habit. When people have their cute new little puppy, they tend to let it pull them all over the place. They think it is kind.

It is not kind.

It's teaching the puppy to damage her throat and neck (you'll learn much more about this in the next book) and to ignore the person on the other end of the lead. Picture this: they have their pup on a lead. The puppy pulls towards something. Their arm stretches out. The puppy pulls harder. With outstretched arm they follow the puppy.

What has this puppy just learnt? "If I pull, they'll follow. And if I pull harder, they'll follow faster!"

For some reason that escapes me, people find this appealing. Once the pup has grown a few months and can get some traction and force, not so much. Then you have the added issue of your dog's reactivity. As a responsible citizen you want to keep your dog under control, so suddenly you start to wind the lead six times round your hand - a dangerous practice in itself - and pull him in tight. This really is not going to work!

Here's an exercise for you to change this entirely. Start this indoors, in a place where your dog feels calm and comfortable. If her anxiety is such that the sight of the lead worries her as she fears she has to go on a walk, work in a room without the "walk" association - the living room, perhaps, or your garden. Whatever gear you usually walk your dog in, work on a soft collar and lead for now. Lots more about kit coming up in Book 2.

Key Lead Skill no.1: Keeping the lead loose

1. Have your dog on a longish lead (6-8 feet, at least 2 metres)
2. Stand still and let the dog pull to the end of the lead, wherever she wants to go
3. Keep your hand close to your hip. Tuck your thumb into your belt if necessary
4. Wait. Wait till the lead slackens the tiniest bit. It doesn't matter why - don't judge. You may think you'll need to wait forever, but it's usually only 20 seconds or so at most
5. As soon as you feel the lead relax - *for any reason at all, even by accident* - call your dog and reward her with a tasty treat at your knee
6. Repeat Steps 2-5 till she understands that it's up to her to keep the lead loose

This exercise is simplicity itself. It tells your dog that you are no longer the one that's pulling. Your hands are soft. It's her choice if she pulls. Given a little time, she'll choose not to pull at all.

If your dog is in the habit of lurching to the end of the lead as soon as it's on, you may have to repeat this exercise frequently. In most cases we need repeat it only long enough to get the new system of lead-holding into our own heads. Once *we've* got it, our dog will get it.

Dogs are doers, not not-doers. So your dog is learning to keep the lead loose, rather than not to pull on it. See the difference?

What you accept is what you get

> ACTION STEP 11:
>
> Every time you put the lead on your dog, you need to remember to keep your hand close to you and wait for her to slacken the lead. If you are in the habit of putting on the lead and letting your dog pull you to the door, then that is what will happen.

What you reward is what you get.

And there are few better rewards for many dogs then heading out through that door! Even your super-anxious dog may pull to the door, as she's on full alert for what she may find the other side - her hormones are racing. Your dog needs to learn that - no matter what happened in the past - things have now changed, which means pulling on the lead will get her nowhere. Dogs aren't dumb. They do what works.

From now on you will never move until the lead is slack.

NEVER!

If you find your arm floating out, recapture it and tuck it into your belt! If it keeps happening, put your partner or one of your children on "arm-watch." They'll love having the chance of pointing out your mistake to you!

In this chapter we have learnt:

- To take a fresh look at things we take for granted
- That building your dog's confidence and connection with you is key
- You can relax
- Your dog can relax
- Anxiety has just been dialled back several notches!

Chapter 10 Dog Body Language

"I'm no threat!"

Unlike us, dogs don't rate vocalisation very highly. Yes - I know that some of us with reactive dogs hear too much of their opinions! But when dogs vocalise it tends to be about their emotional state - fear, excitement, alarm, pain, and so on. When they want to "speak" to each other, they use their highly sophisticated and silent body language.

And if we want a chance of joining in this conversation, we need to learn this powerful lingo! There are some terrific visual resources that help you to understand what your dog is saying, and you'll find some good ones in the Resources Section.

Body signals can be large or tiny. For instance a slow blink of the eyes is a calming signal. Staring is rude - not just in dogs! - and while a dog may need to look at another dog to study whether that dog is a threat or not, they should not do it in a threatening way.

Imagine this: you're sitting on a bus, and the man opposite you has an enormous nose. You feel the need to study this extraordinary nose, so you choose a moment when he's looking away to have a peer at it. Then he looks back towards you. You quickly focus on the shop you can see past his shoulder, or your watch - anything to demonstrate that you weren't staring at him!

Dogs will do the same thing - they'll slow-blink their eyes to break their stare, they'll start sniffing the ground, they'll turn and look somewhere else, or they'll turn their whole body away. The last two are called a "lookaway" and once you start noticing your dog doing lookaways you'll know that there is something she's avoiding looking at. This could be a strange dog, a strange dog staring at her, a person, whatever creature or thing worries her.

At the same time as looking away, or sniffing the ground, your dog can keep the worrying thing in her peripheral vision. Dogs have 270° vision, as against our measly 180° range. So they can turn their head right away - lessening any sign of conflict - while still remaining able to study the other dog or person. This is clearly an essential survival skill.

Two lookaways

There are other signs you'll be looking out for, such as lip-licking, yawning, shaking-off, which all indicate anxiety. The shaking-off is settling the coat down again after the hairs have all stood on end - just like us when we get a fright, have goose bumps, then do a quick shiver to snap out of it. It's a sign that the dog *was* alarmed and anxious, but has decided to move on.

A quick dart of the tongue as a lip-lick, when it's not to do with food, is a calming signal. It tells the other dog that he's a little bit worried. Yawning is also more associated with release of tension - a sign that the dog *was* tense.

Tail-wagging is much misunderstood. There is a whole language of the tail! Dogs will even wag their tail to one side when they greet someone they know. And of course there are variables depending on the type of dog and type of tail (some dogs, like terriers, carry their tails very straight and erect a lot of the time). Many is the person who has been bitten by a dog whose tail was wagging! A wagging tail is simply evidence of agitation in the dog.

The elevation of the tail and the speed of wagging have a lot to do with it. Think soppy Golden Retriever with sinuous body movement, soft eyes, mouth slack and open, tongue lolling, and mid-height gently waving tail, as the epitome of the friendly dog. Think fierce Doberman with tall, stiff, erect body, stiff tail, leaning forward, straight legs, mouth shut, staring eyes, frown, frozen position - move calmly away from this dog without looking at him.

Yes - before my inbox explodes with protests - there are lovely, friendly Dobermans, and there are Golden Retrievers who bite. I'm giving you an example of what the typical body language is saying in a breed you should recognise. Dobermans have been bred to look fierce as they are wanted as guard dogs, so breeders have selected for these traits.

Grinning with eyes closed: some dogs will do this to show that they mean no harm. It's what you see in those dreadful internet videos about "guilty" dogs. More often than not, the dog has no idea why their owner is cross with them, and they're saying "Please don't punish me". It's pretty pathetic that people set this up, video it, then put the video online to laugh at the unfortunate dog.

You may notice the tense lines around the mouth and cheeks - especially if you have a smooth-coated dog. His ears may be doing a dance, and running through several signals in succession. Some dogs will move into slow motion, maybe creeping on their belly. Some will dangle a front paw puppy-style to show they're no threat. Not every dog does every single signal, but they will run through a sequence of them, from a little bit anxious right up to "Get me outa here!", which is one step away from a bite.

Bites

Dogs never "bite out of the blue". There's always been a procession of signs that show the dog's increasing discomfort. Trouble is, unsocialised dogs and humans tend not to be able to read them. This is the reason for all those heart-stoppingly gruesome internet videos of babies crawling over dogs and pulling their ears. Some of those babies are a whisker away from getting bitten. Some do get bitten - then guess whose fault it is? And the doting parents see none of the dog's discomfort and allow all sorts of intrusions into the dog's dignity. The poor dog is trapped! He's saying,

- Look away = Please don't come near me
- Moving away = I wish I could get away from you
- Blink = I'm not a threat to you
- Lip-lick = This is worrying - where's my escape route?
- Stiff body = This should show them I'm not in the mood
- Staring with whites of eyes showing = I'm really *really* not happy about this
- Wrinkling lip = Would you just leave me alone?
- Growl = I'm serious - leave me alone! (see Chapter 6)
- Snap = Look! I have teeth! I will use them if I have to!
- Bite = I told you 9 times to clear off. Why didn't you get the message?

Breed variations

Not all dogs are the same shape, size, or coat-type. And clearly these things can make a difference. A short-coated dog's signs are in general much easier to read.

If your dog is arousing a lot of suspicion in other dogs, there may be something you can do to help. If he has a mop of hair over his eyes, trim it! Be sure he can see clearly. If you were in a frightening situation, you wouldn't want to be trying to look through a thick veil! My Border Collie, Rollo, when young, had what I thought a very fetching curled-up coat over his shoulders. The hair swept up and forward instead of lying back flat. This could be misconstrued by another dog as raised hackles - a sign of fear or aggression in a dog, who is standing his hair up to make himself look as big as possible. So we took to smoothing his coat down before meeting other dogs.

An unwarranted intrusion

I watched a scene once where a street-dog was happily moving amongst the crowds at a fair, snuffling the ground for food and minding his own business. A woman spotted him, put on a daft smile, and silently reached down and scratched his bum. The dog spun round with a bark, before moving off and looking for food elsewhere. "That dog nearly bit me!" the woman complained loudly to whoever would listen. Dogs are so quick: if he'd wanted to bite her she would have been bitten! This dog was simply telling her to clear off.

And in my view the dog was quite justified. How would she have felt if a stranger had put on a silly expression, then scratched *her* bum? I bet she'd have had something to say!

Dogs are not our playthings. They are sentient beings with their own opinions and feelings. We expect them to fit into our lives, for our benefit. The least we can do is have some understanding of what they are thinking, feeling - and saying.

Honour your dog!

As you espouse choice-based training, you are going to find that your dog can manage situations rather better than you thought - if you let her get on with it! Of course, you need to keep everyone safe, and if your dog has bitten then your first priority is to ensure it can't happen again - more about that in the next book.

But for now, you want to encourage her to express her body language freely. This means your lead must be loose so that she *can!* She can't look calm and relaxed when her head is being held up and she can't breathe properly. When you see a dog or person or whatever alarms her, you can relax your hands on your loose lead and watch what your dog does. She may stare at them for a bit, then turn her head back to you and say "Can we go now?" Perfect! Off you both go, without anyone having got upset. If she starts to get taller and stiffer, creeps forward, shuts her mouth - or any of the other signs you will now recognise, then that's when you decide to go, and take her happily with you.

ACTION STEP 12:

Research Dog Body Language thoroughly and start spotting what your dog is saying and when. Check out the Resources Section for where to look. Notice the signals he uses and those he doesn't - and when you see them in another dog. Start to notice your reactive dog's signals earlier and earlier so that you can catch the moment he seems unhappy about another dog or person or rattly plastic bag and relieve the tension by removing him from the scene.

In this chapter we have:

- Had an immersion course in a foreign language
- Learned to respect our dog's opinions
- Remembered that it's all about choice - give your dog a choice, and applaud a good choice

Chapter 11 Health aspects

Neutering

This chapter is all about the physical side of your dog. I'll start off with the thorny subject of neutering. Remember, I'm not a vet, so we are only interested here in the effects neutering may or may not have on our dog's reactivity and state of mind. And these effects can be major! So I'm not looking at neutering as a population control strategy, neutering which is essential for some medical reason, or neutering as a convenience option for the owner. Nor am I looking at the evidence which shows increased medical and orthopaedic issues associated with neutering - especially early neutering (anything before age 1, roughly speaking).

And if your dog is already neutered, don't skip this section! It may explain a few things for you, and you need to know for your next dog.

Myth: neutering will calm my dog down

Neutering will remove certain body parts from your dog which will stop the flow of the associated hormones through the body. Your dog will no longer be able to reproduce, and will not be driven by sexual urges *as much*. A neutered male may still mount and tie with a bitch on heat - he's just firing blanks. Neutered dogs as well as entire dogs and bitches can still get sexually excited by the presence of a bitch in season, which is why bitches on heat are not allowed at competitions which require focus from the competitors, such as Obedience, Dancing with Dogs, and so on. Most dog training classes will not take a bitch in season - even if all the other dogs in the class are female or neutered. Too exciting!

If your dog is an escapologist and a rambler at the moment, and you think that that is a sexually-driven activity, neutering will only take the edge off his enthusiasm. If you want his habits to change you need to apply some training to the problem. In other words, neutering is not a quick fix, though it may well be a good step in this case.

Nor will it "calm down" your young dog, who is behaving as … a young dog. Possibly just a young dog in need of training. In fact, studies have shown that the opposite is true! Your neutered dog or bitch is apparently likely to be *more* excitable than an intact dog.

Myth: neutering will make my dog less aggressive

And this is the big one, and our focus in these books. It has been shown, in a number of recent scientific studies, that neutering - especially early neutering - *will increase sound sensitivity, touch sensitivity, fears, and aggression*, in both males and females. In some cases that increase is "significant" or "highly significant". People-directed aggression in females, for instance, was significantly elevated in the neutered bitches studied. (See the Resources Section for chapter and verse on this.) That's what those studies found. A lot more research is needed to get more answers, and these studies can take years to produce reliable results.

These unfortunate outcomes are - of course - not guaranteed to happen if you neuter your dog! But it's important to be aware that they just may happen. And if they complicate an already complicated situation, that's not helpful.

Neutering has the potential to make your dog worse.

Isn't this a social obligation?

There are cultural differences across the globe. In some cultures neutering is referred to as "getting the dog fixed" - as if the dog has arrived in some way faulty and needs repair. In fact in such cultures it's rare to find unneutered dogs except those earmarked for breeding or those belonging to people who couldn't care less.

On the other hand, there are plenty of cultures where it's normal to leave dogs entire, even mixed-sex dogs in the same household. In some European countries it is considered barbaric to mutilate dogs, and neutering of either sex is usually only done for medical reasons. At the other extreme we have cultures where people are vociferous in declaring that all dogs should be neutered and it is our duty as a citizen to do this.

Those who decide to neuter as a means of population control are often the ones who would not leave their dog straying anyway. Those who don't care, don't care. So it's pretty inefficient at preventing unwanted puppies - just look at the bulging shelters. If you are able to manage a household of unneutered dogs without mishap (as many breeders do), then you will have more freedom in your choice. Naturally, any litters resulting from your intact dogs should be carefully planned. Finding the right homes for puppies can be a daunting task. Being able to adopt this strategy may depend on your individual dog - some can be very determined to find a mate!

So I'm simply suggesting that you need to change your mindset from neutering being an automatic next step for your puppy to seeing that you have a choice in this.

The one unarguable fact of neutering is that it is irreversible. So any changes made cannot be unmade. If neutering your reactive dog causes his or her reactivity to double in frequency and intensity, you are now up the creek without a paddle. There is no way back.

A halfway house could be veterinary intervention in the form of "chemical castration" or drugs which control the extreme symptoms some bitches experience, such as false pregnancies, extended and irregular seasons. Such interventions are temporary and may be worth looking into with your vet to see how behaviour is affected.

Young and cautious or fearful males *can* become very aggressive in appearance when their source of testosterone dries up overnight.

Females *can* become unpredictable after neutering - especially if there were complications seen earlier, like becoming very spooky or reactive before a season, or having difficult false pregnancies.

Whatever you decide to do with your dog's sexual status, please look into the literature carefully first. Do not listen to the old wives' tales about neutering "calming the dog down". *This step is irreversible!* If you find things have got worse after neutering, there is now no way back.

In case you think I am on a mission to ban neutering, I can tell you that only one of my four dogs is entire at the time of writing. You have to decide what is right for your situation. I just want you to realise that there's more to this than meets the eye, and *you do have a choice.*

If you have already neutered your dog, don't waste energy on recriminations or what-ifs. It's water under the bridge. As ever, we'll work with what we have right now.

(IN)ACTION STEP 13:

If your dog is still entire, study the literature before taking this step. As you are reading this book and have presumably already got a problem of fear or aggression, *don't neuter right now.* You have plenty of time later to do this, if it's the right decision for your dog. *Purely from a behavioural point of view,* do not neuter a reactive bitch before her second season, and do not neuter a reactive dog till he is mature (2-3 years old, depending on breed). Wait till you have worked through this program then see how he or she is. Remember you need to discuss all this with a vet!

Medications

There are a number of meds that may help your dog, many developed from those used for psychological problems in humans. If your dog's fears and reactivity are so severe that he cannot lead a normal life, then a visit to a veterinary behaviourist is indicated. Apart from fear of strangers and/or strange dogs, these fears may include OCD (Obsessive Compulsive Disorders) like stalking and chasing lights, shadows, or reflections; extreme Separation Anxiety which causes physical damage to the dog; extreme fear of storms or traffic, for instance, which cause panic and danger.

There are a few questions you need to ask your vet before you embark on a course of prescribed medication for your dog:

1. How long will it be before it takes effect? This can be weeks or months.
2. Can I stop the medication abruptly or must the dog be weaned off it?
3. What known side-effects are there?

Many prescription medications have side-effects. Steroids, for instance - often prescribed for skin problems - are known to cause an increase in aggression in some dogs. See if there is an alternative you can use.

While you're at the vet, check out thyroid imbalance and pain. Who doesn't feel aggressive when suffering from earache or toothache? Not to mention a twinge in your back or hips that gets you every time someone touches you! Some touch sensitivity can be an early symptom of serious illness.

Some people think that using medication for their dog is in some way an admission of failure on their part. If the dog is helped by medication, then go for it! Would you deny this help to your child? It's not a moral issue - it just is as it is.

Over-the-counter medications

There is a whole slew of OTC remedies available, from herbal mixtures to flower remedies. Check with your vet that they can do no harm, then give them a go. For some dogs they work brilliantly, for others not at all.

There are quick-acting remedies, often marketed for fear of fireworks. And I have found Bach flower remedies work fast (if they're going to work at all).

ACTION STEP 14:

If you haven't yet booked that vet check suggested in Chapter 4, get onto it now!

Other therapies

There are many canine therapists now available to help your dog, for example:

- TTouch (previously known as Tellington Touch)
- Canine Massage
- Bowen Technique

These all use touching techniques which ease your dog's body (and therefore mind), uncover any hidden or intermittent pain points, and can improve body balance (and therefore mental balance too).

TTouch is known for its superb calming abilities. I have seen frantic and anxious dogs reduced to a sighing furry stretched-out heap on the floor after a skilled practitioner has spent a few minutes "hitting the spot".

It's well worth seeking out a local accredited practitioner and see how it goes for your dog. This is not New Age woolliness - they have governing bodies and exams: see the Resources Section. Some people find the therapies so effective for their precious dog (or cat or parrot or you-name-it) that they go on to study and qualify as a practitioner themselves.

In this chapter we have learnt that:

- Neutering may make your reactive, fearful dog worse
- This step cannot be undone
- Medication may help
- Canine touch therapies are very likely to help - and be very popular with your dog!

Conclusion

So now you know!

- You have a far greater understanding of what's going on and why
- You are no longer blaming your dog
- You are no longer blaming your dog's history
- You are no longer blaming yourself!
- and, understandable as it may be, you know it's pointless blaming those who misled you in the past

Furthermore, you are now on the road to some solid changes which will make a world of difference to the both of you. You can see your dog with new eyes, you can show empathy with her, and you can face the future together.

One student said to me when arriving for her second session, that if they had been at the stage they now were with their dog, they wouldn't have needed to call me out. In other words, just working on the information in this first book made a massive difference to the way they understood their dog and why he was doing what he was doing.

With understanding comes love and patience. Patience, love, and encouragement will be needed in spades in the next two books! You can make dramatic changes in your dog's worldview - but it isn't an overnight fix. You'll be taking a couple of steps forward, then one back, a lot of the time. Provided you keep your eyes on your end goal, you'll get there.

And what is your end goal? It should be simple - and perhaps not what you thought when you embarked on this program! Your dog does not have to be everyone's friend. She may enjoy the company of some dog-friends she knows well, or she may say - like my Lacy aka Greta Garbo - "I want to be alone". (Garbo actually said she wanted to be "let alone", which is even more to the point.) Some of us love parties and some of us hate them - allow your dog to choose what camp she is comfortable in, and honour her decision.

A practical and sensible goal would be for your dog to feel happier and more confident when out, for you to have techniques and tricks up your sleeve to cope with any eventuality, and for you both to enjoy your walks - both on-lead on the street, and off-lead in the safety of forest and wide open spaces.

Head to Book 2: **Change for your Growly Dog!** *Action steps to build confidence in your fearful, aggressive, or reactive dog* and let's get to it!

Appreciation

I want to offer thanks to all those who have helped me get where I am in my life with dogs:

- First of all, my own long-suffering dogs! They have taught me so much when I've taken the time to listen.
- My reactive dog Lacy who is a star and has opened up a new world for me.
- My students, who have shown me how they learn best, enabling me to give them what they need to know in a way that works for them.
- Some legendary teachers, principal amongst them: Sue Ailsby, Leslie McDevitt, Grisha Stewart, Chirag Patel, Susan Garrett. I wholeheartedly recommend them. They are trailblazers.

Resources

You know now that there's light at the end of this tunnel! And to discover that the tunnel is much shorter than you think, get the next two parts of the puzzle here:

Essential Skills for your *Growly* but Brilliant Family Dog series
Book 2 **Change for your Growly Dog!** *Action steps to build confidence in your fearful, aggressive, or reactive dog*
Book 3 **Calm walks with your Growly Dog** *Strategies and techniques for your fearful, aggressive, or reactive dog*

For a very thorough, in-depth, approach, where I will be on hand to answer all your questions, go to

brilliantfamilydog.teachable.com

where you'll find info about the online course which takes all this to the next level, giving you personal support and encouragement as well as all the lessons and techniques you need to change your life with your Growly Dog.

For a free taster course: **www.brilliantfamilydog.com/growly**

And for loads of articles on Growly Dogs and Choice Training, go to **www.brilliantfamilydog.com** where you'll also find a course on solving everyday dog and puppy problems.

You'll also find the **Essential Skills for a Brilliant Family Dog** series of e-books helpful. Take a holistic view of your relationship with your dog and work on new skills inside the house as well as when you're out. If your dog has always had to be kept on lead because you were afraid he was not safe, you'll definitely need Book 4 for your new life!

Book 1 Calm Down! *Step-by-Step to a Calm, Relaxed, and Brilliant Family Dog*
Book 2 Leave it! *How to teach Amazing Impulse Control to your Brilliant Family Dog*
Book 3 Let's Go! *Enjoy Companionable Walks with your Brilliant Family Dog*
Book 4 Here Boy! *Step-by-step to a Stunning Recall from your Brilliant Family Dog*

And you'll be pleased to know that Book 1 is currently free at all e-book stores!

Here are the links to all the resources mentioned in this book:

Books by other authors:

I'll Be Home Soon: How to Prevent and Treat Separation Anxiety by Patricia McConnell, pub First Stone, 2010

Control Unleashed: Creating a Focused and Confident Dog by Leslie McDevitt, pub Clean Run Productions LLC, 2007
http://controlunleashed.net/book.html

Behavior Adjustment Training 2.0: New Practical Techniques for Fear, Frustration, and Aggression in Dogs by Grisha Stewart, pub Dogwise Publishing, 2016

Websites:

www.muzzleupproject.com - all things muzzle

www.goodfordogs.co.uk/products - Wiggles Wags and Whiskers Freedom Harness - UK and Europe [This is me. If you buy from me I will benefit financially, but it won't cost you any more.]

http://2houndswholesale.com/Where-to-Buy.html - Wiggles Wags and Whiskers Freedom Harness - rest of the world

https://www.youtube.com/watch?v=1OHEB41yRdU - one of many calming sound recordings

https://positively.com/dog-wellness/dog-enrichment/music-for-dogs/canine-noise-phobia-series/ - for desensitisation

http://en.turid-rugaas.no/calming-signals---the-art-of-survival.html - dog body language

http://www.youtube.com/watch?v=00_9JPltXHI - dog body language

http://www.youtube.com/watch?v=bstvG_SUzMo - dog body language

http://www.doggiedrawings.net/#!freeposters/ckm8 - Lili Chin's fantastic dog body language illustrations. Please respect her requests re sharing her copyright material - she is very generous

http://www.kendalshepherd.com/the-canine-commandments/ - The Canine Ladder of Aggression

www.hemopet.org - Dr Jean Dodds, authority on Hypothyroidism and dog allergies

www.allaboutdogfood.co.uk Independent UK reference for what's really in that bag

www.rawmeatybones.com A vet shows you how to get started on a raw diet

Force-free training hubs:

http://www.apdt.co.uk/dog-owners/local-dog-trainers - UK resource for force-free trainers

http://www.petprofessionalguild.com/PetGuildMembers - global resource for force-free trainers

http://grishastewart.com/cbati-directory/ - global resource for specialist Certified BAT Instructors

Neutering resources quoted:

http://www.thelabradorsite.com/should-i-have-my-labrador-neutered-the-latest-evidence/ - The effects of neutering on health and behaviour: a summary
Accessed 2016

http://www.atftc.com/health/SNBehaviorBoneDataSnapShot.pdf
Behavioral and Physical Effects of Spaying and Neutering Domestic Dogs (Canis familiaris)
Summary of findings detailed in a Masters thesis submitted to and accepted by Hunter College
by Parvene Farhoody in May, 2010
Accessed 2016

http://www.caninesports.com/uploads/1/5/3/1/15319800/vizsla_javma_study.pdf
AVMA, Vol 244, No. 3, February 1, 2014
Evaluation of the risk and age of onset of cancer and behavioral disorders in gonadectomized Vizslas
M. Christine Zink DVM PhD, Parvene Farhoody MA, Samra E. Elser BS, Lynda D. Ruffini, Tom A. Gibbons MS, Randall H. Rieger PhD
Accessed 2016

http://saova.org/articles/Early%20SN%20and%20Behavior.pdf
Non-reproductive Effects of Spaying and Neutering on Behavior in Dogs
Deborah L. Duffy PhD, and James A. Serpell PhD
Center for the Interaction of Animals and Society, School of Veterinary Medicine, University of Pennsylvania
Accessed 2016

Alternative practitioner societies:
www.ttouch.com
www.ttouchteam.co.uk
www.k9-massageguild.co.uk
www.massageawareness.com
www.caninebowentechnique.com

Don't go without your free book!

Impulse Control is particularly valuable for the reactive and anxious dog. Get a head start with your training by developing astonishing self-control in your dog! Change your dog from quick on the trigger, to thoughtful and reflective.

Go now and get your step-by-step book absolutely free at
Brilliant Family Dog
www.brilliantfamilydog.com/freebook-growly

About the author

I've been training dogs for many years. First for competitive dog sports and over time to be stellar family pets. For most of my life, I've lived with up to four dogs, so I'm well used to getting a multi-dog household to run smoothly. It soon became clear that a force-free approach was by far the most successful, effective, and rewarding for me and the dogs. I've done the necessary studying for my various qualifications - for rehab of anxious and fearful "aggressive" dogs, early puppy development, and learning theory and its practical applications. I am continually studying and learning this endlessly amazing subject!

There are some superb teachers and advocates of force-free dog training, and you'll find those I am particularly indebted to in the Appreciation Section. Some of the methods I show you are well-known in the force-free dog training community, while many have my own particular twist.

A lot of my learning has come through the Puppy Classes, Puppy Walks, and Growly Dog Courses I teach. These dog-owners are not looking for competition-standard training; they just want a Brilliant Family Dog they can take anywhere. It's a particular joy for me to see a Growly Dog who arrived at the first session a reactive bundle of nerves and fear, who ends up able to cope with almost anything the world chucks his way - becoming a relaxed and happy dog with a confident owner in the process.

Working with real dogs and their real owners keeps me humble - and resourceful! It's no good being brilliant at training dogs if you can't convey this enthusiasm and knowledge to the person the dog has to live with. So I'm grateful for everything my students have taught me about how they learn best.

Beverley Courtney BA(Hons) CBATI CAP2 MAPDT(UK) PPG
www.brilliantfamilydog.com

Printed in Great Britain
by Amazon

25449278R00063